Secrets of the Well

Shane Warren

Secrets of the Well

Shane Warren

Printed in the United States of America

ISBN # 978-1-60458-549-0

Secrets of the Well

For Additional Information

Email: pastorshane@firstassemblywm.org

DEDICATION

I dedicate this book to Pam, my beautiful wife and best friend, for her unwavering support and love during our twenty years of marriage and ministry,

To my wonderful son Adam of whom I am very proud, you bring me great joy,

To the memory of my late father and mother, Don and Linda Warren and my grandparents, James and Dorothy Warren. Thank you for pushing me into my destiny. Soon we will rejoice together in eternity!

Also, to my church family, thank you for the opportunity to serve as your pastor and for the freedom to pursue God's highest call for my life.

INTRODUCTION

I have led worship for sixteen years and have walked through many cycles, seasons, and reformations. I have served as worship leader for Pastor Shane Warren for six of those years. I have grown immensely while serving under this man of God. It is an incredible honor to partner with him in the celebration of his first book.

I am convinced that a church can worship only at the level where the Pastor leads and lives. Pastor Shane Warren leads and lives the lifestyle of a true worshipper. We share a spiritual connection that bonds us beyond a song list on Sunday mornings. The Lord has fashioned us together by the power of the Holy Spirit to be unified arms extended to lead people into the presence of God.

I am personally adopting this book as my **textbook on worship.** I am fully persuaded that *leaders are learners.* If you are a spiritual leader in any capacity, this book will impart to you manifold revelation and insight into the power and warfare of worship. You will be spiritually invigorated as you learn the precepts and scriptural principles Pastor Shane Warren declares in this book.

I have always told myself and those who serve with me in worship ministry: "Worship is a school from which we never graduate." This book will allow you to increase in knowledge, focus your spirit and equip you with potent weapons that will overcome, drive away, and defeat your adversary. I can tell you first hand how potent these weapons are. I am reminded of a service in 2007 when the congregation at The Assembly in West Monroe, Louisiana, was in the midst of a powerful prophetic worship service. None of the musicians were playing and no one was singing. From the platform where I stood, I noticed a man in the audience to my left whom we knew as the "blind man." During this glorious time of worship, he gripped his walking stick and purposefully approached the altar area. Pastor was on the platform charging the people to be filled with the Holy Spirit. Among the hundreds of voices that were raised in worship, I heard three words that echoed above the crowd. "I can see!" "I can see!" As the sound of voices roared in worship, the "blind man" had been instantly healed of total blindness. To this day, the doctor's report proves that he has no nerves connected to the interior of his eyes, **but he can see!** Hallelujah!

Pastor Warren teaches that physical signs are also a spiritual reflection. I believe the church has been blind to the real reason for worship for far too long. We have eyes, but we have no vision or sight of why we worship. Just as did the "blind man," **if we will purposefully approach God, He will purposefully impart**! This book will remove the lid from your current worship relationship with the Lord and impart new wine that will increase the capacity for anointing in your life. I honestly believe that this book will take you through the following three phases:

1. Separation. I believe that we confuse the word *separation* with the term *isolation*. When Jesus was led into the dessert, He was not isolated. He was not apart from God. He was separated only from nominal influences. I beg you to allow the Lord to separate you from nominal influences while you read this book. Refuse to be an isolated worshipper that holds onto methods and preferences.

2. Revitalization. As you read this book, scriptural perspectives that cannot be compromised will challenge you. Your worship relationship will shed old wine skins and put on a new garment of praise.

3. Maximization. Allow the Lord to remove old unproductive habits and thought patterns concerning worship. **Increase always brings release**. This book will enable you to maximize your understanding and weaponry of worship. It is the will of God that your cup

run over, not just in blessings, but it spiritual revelation as well.

Prepare yourself for a great journey and expect God to shake everything that can be shaken until that which remains is of Him. Get ready. Warfare is about to begin. You are walking into the lines of battle. Take your position and listen to the voice of the Holy Spirit as He imparts strategic battle plans into your spirit.

Brad Jackson, Minister of Music
First Assembly of God
West Monroe, Louisiana

CONTENTS

Chapter 1

When an Altar Becomes a Well

I am always amazed at the mercy of the Lord. He continually reaches to us with arms of love and compassion. Even when our lives are totally wrecked by our own wickedness, Jesus is still moved with compassion on our behalf. It is this unchanging, overwhelming love that is the backdrop to one of the most powerful passages in the entire Bible on the subject of worship.

In John 4 Jesus feels the strong leading of the Holy Spirit to go through a place called Samaria. Because the Pharisees were trying to incite competition between Jesus and John the Baptist (John 3:25-30), Jesus had left Judea and started north for Galilee, where he spent over eighty percent of his ministerial time. He could have taken several routes to arrive at his destination: along the coast, across the Jordan and up through Perea, or *straight* through Samaria. These routes were well traveled and well known in Jesus' day. However, Orthodox Jews almost always avoided Samaria because of a long-standing, deep-seated hatred for the Samaritan people.

The Samaritans were considered a mixed race--part Jew and part Gentile. During the Assyrian captivity of the ten northern tribes in 727 B.C., there was the intermarrying of Jews with Gentiles who naturally produced offspring. Because of their captivity, many could not prove their genealogy and were thus rejected by Orthodox communities. At that time Samaritans established their own temple and religious services at Mt. Gerizim. This practice incited greater despite for the Samaritan people because they appeared to the Orthodox to be insulting the Temple services of Jerusalem. The fires of prejudice were so great toward the Samaritan people that Pharisees would actually pray that no Samaritan would be raised in the resurrection. A Jew was

> **Abraham had built an *altar* of *worship* that became a *well* of *resource*.**

considered unclean if he had the dust of Samaria on his feet! In fact, when the enemies of Jesus wanted to insult Him and His ministry they would call Him a Samaritan (John 8:48).

The wonderful thing about Jesus is that He was not controlled by the cultural nuances of the day; instead, most of His actions were completely counter-cultural for that era. He had a remarkable ability to reach across racial, religious and socio-economic lines; this ability is what made and continues to make Him *relevant to every generation*. Contrary to popular pulpiteering, Jesus has never had a problem being relevant to the world: He is the *"same yesterday, today and forever..."* (Hebrews 13:8). One of the greatest needs in the body of Christ today is for the church to rediscover its identity in an unchanging, relevant Jesus and not be moved with every wind or fad of the times. This story in John 4 is one of those instances of Jesus' ministry relevance that is counter-cultural! Jesus was on a divinely appointed schedule that made it necessary for Him to travel through Samaria. Why? There was a woman there that needed a revelation encounter that would change her life.

He arrived at Jacob's Well at the *sixth hour*, about twelve noon. The normal time for women to fetch water was either early in the morning or late in the afternoon. The disciples had gone into town to the grocery store while Jesus waited at the well. The scripture says that Jesus was weary from the journey and sat down on Jacob's Well. It was there that he encountered a woman whose life desperately needed a healing touch. Before getting any deeper into this story, a little known truth about Jacob's Well must be established.

Genesis 12:5-7 records that *"Abram took Sarai his wife, and Lot his brother's son, and all their substance that they had gathered, and the souls that they had gotten in Haran; and they went forth to go into the land of Canaan; and into the land of Canaan they came. And Abram passed through the land unto the place of Sichem, unto the plain of Moreh. And the Canaanite was then in the land. And the Lord appeared unto Abram, and said, 'Unto thy seed will I give this land: and there builded he an altar unto the Lord, who appeared unto him.'"* God had promised Abram a land; and as he moved into the land, he came to a place called Sichem (also known as Sychar).

It was at Sichem that God confirmed his promise to Abraham; so Abraham built an altar to worship God there. It is interesting that Sichem is not mentioned in the life of Isaac, Abraham's son, at all; rather it skipped a generation and was mentioned in Jacob's life, Abraham's grandson. Genesis 33:18 states that Jacob came to Sichem, and there he built another altar. Then, in Joshua 24:32 Joseph, Jacob's son, was buried in Shechem-- same place--in a parcel of ground that Jacob bought for one hundred pieces of silver. The name of Sicham, Shechem or Sychar, is mentioned numerous times after that throughout the Old Testament. However, the New Testament in John 4:5 says *"Then cometh he to a city of Samaria, which is called Sychar, near to the parcel of ground that Jacob gave to his son Joseph. Now Jacob's well was there."* Abraham had built an altar of *worship* that became a *well* of resource.

In fact, we find this secret within the word *worship* itself. The origins of the word *worship* come from the Anglo-Saxon compound word *weorthscype*. *Weorth* means *worth, value, or respect;* and *scype* means *to shape or to build*; therefore, *worship* is by definition *the shaping or building of worth value and respect.* Psalms 22:3 says, *"You sit as the Holy One. The praises of Israel are your throne"* (NCV). When we worship, we are building God a seat to sit upon! Just as the Ark of the Covenant provided a Mercy Seat for God to sit upon; so also our praise creates a place for Him to sit.

I Discovered a Well

Abraham's building an altar of worship created an opportunity for another generation to be resourced by revelation. The well was not just a place to draw water; it was a place of worship! Beloved, one of the most powerful principles that I have ever learned is that worship is a mighty resource. I have personally discovered this truth for myself. My father, once a very successful entrepreneur, became very ill and as a result died a pauper. Most of my adult life, I watched my hero suffer terribly at the hands of physicians only to lose the battle at the age of fifty-seven. On the heels of his death, my mother, who took care of him for over eighteen years, was overcome by grief and illness as well. I lost my precious mother at the age of fifty-seven, three years after my father's death. She suffered terribly and literally died of starvation because of medications and grief. In the final months of her life, my brother and I took turns trying to help her and trying to pull her out of the clutches of death. At one point she was staying in our home under hospice care.

Those were definitely the saddest days of my life. They were filled with restless nights as I soaked my pillow with tears. Night after night I lay in bed with my arms wrapped around my mother's frail sixty-pound body pleading with God for her health and life. At that time I could not talk about her condition, and we did not have much fellowship with people because she was uncomfortable with groups. Late one night, literally at the end of my emotional, physical and financial rope, I got up out of bed at 10:30 p. m., and went to a small room in our home where I kept an electric guitar. I have always wished I could play well, but I am not very good. Putting the guitar around my neck, I said these words to God, "God, I don't blame you for my mother's condition. I don't understand. I am a man of faith and prayer. Many times I have laid my hands on people and have seen them instantly healed. I have watched blinded eyes open in my services and observed deaf ears miraculously hear. I have prayed and believed for my mother, and now I am empty. There are no more words for prayer and supplication. The only thing I have left is my song of worship, and I refuse to let Satan or any questionable circumstances take that! So, tonight I am going to turn this amp up and play unto You because I don't have anything else to give."

As I began to play, I felt the presence of God invade the atmosphere of my house, especially that little room. At one point I lost track of time and place and felt as if I were being carried to the *high places of the earth* (Deuteronomy 32:13-15). Out of the heavenlies came joy that replaced my sorrow and strength that replaced my weakness. Unfathomable peace took hold of my mind as the glory of God like a cloud enveloped me. All that came to mind is the scripture in Luke 4 which states that when Jesus' temptation had ended *"angels came and ministered to him...."* I could physically feel the resource of heaven making deposits in my bankrupt soul. When I came to myself, I was sitting in my chair in that room with my guitar around my neck. The clock read 6:00 a. m. For almost seven hours, I had been translated into a different realm as the Lord ministered to me in my weakest moment.

The Throne Room Is Waiting!

The next morning as I joined my staff in prayer at 9:00 a. m., I inquired of the Lord, "What happened last night?" He gently whispered to my spirit, "You built an altar of worship to me, and I made it a well of resource for you." From that day forward, I have made my way nightly into that little secret place and soared into the heavenlies on the wings of worship. Since that time there have been more sad, lonely hard days; however, each time that I build the altar of worship my strength is renewed, my fears are swept way, and I receive numerous revelation keys that unlock the heavens over my life and ministry.

From that experience, as did the Samaritan woman that Jesus met, I have found many *resources at the well of worship.* In the subsequent chapters of this book, I am going to reveal the secrets that I have found at the well with the Lord. Whatever you do, do not stop reading! I believe there are some keys woven within the pages of this book that could very well turn your life around to the glory of God and unleash the abundance of heaven on your behalf. However, before you read another word, I dare you to take the next fifteen to thirty minutes to find a quiet place and to start to worship. I have asked God to give you the same Throne-Room experience that I had before you finish this book! Build the altar of worship and find your resources now! They cannot be found in the arm of flesh; they can be found only as you soar to the high places of the earth through worship. Allow the wings of worship to use your winds of turmoil to take you out of this earthly atmosphere into a heavenly one.

Chapter 2

Secrets of the Well

This Samaritan woman is drawing water in the middle of the day, which is highly unusual behavior for a woman of her day and culture. Of course, we quickly learn from the conversation in John 4:6-24 that there are probably some good reasons for her untimely appearance at the well. No doubt, she was suffering, as are so many of us, from the oppression of past failures and her current questionable lifestyle. Little did she know that she was about to receive a key that would change her life forever.

> **"When I worship, I would rather my heart be without words than my words be without heart."**
>
> Lamar Boschman

This visit to the well was unlike all the previous visits. Normally, she would make her way to the well in the middle of the day to avoid the scrutiny, jeers, and rejection of the other women. Jesus noted that she was not an expert on relationships at all. She had suffered the pain of five divorces and currently was living out of wedlock with a sixth man. Maybe she did not come to the well with the other women because her choices in life had shamed her to the point that she could not bear being the laughing stock of the community. Perhaps her heart could not take other women's questioning her about her multiple relationships in a society that highly valued monogamy at all costs. Possibly her having to explain five major failures and to make excuses for her current lifestyle was just too much to bear emotionally. Plus, with every explanation the wounds of relationships-gone-bad were reopened like a botched surgery that never heals. Since the community had isolated her, she had also isolated herself for her own emotional protection. These are the reasons she is at the well in the middle of the day. It is at Jacob's Well that she finds a Jew sitting who immediately asks her for a drink of water. Knowing the strained relationships between Samaritans and Jews, she questions the Lord's motives.

At this point I must admit that of all of the people in the Bible a woman of this character would not have been my personal choice to whom to reveal the greatest revelation of worship in the New Testament; but the Lord *"...sees not as man sees, for man looks at the **outward appearance**, but the LORD looks at the heart"* (1 Samuel 16:7). Jesus' prophetic eyes must have seen a desire for breakthrough in the heart of this woman. In His mercy the Lord gave her a key that changed her life, healed her brokenness, and removed her shame – the key of *worship*.

As previously stated, the Samaritans had built their own temple so they could worship God as the Orthodox Jews worshipped in Jerusalem. At this point the story takes an interesting turn. Once Jesus identifies her condition, He immediately starts teaching her about worship. Get this picture in your mind: He is sitting on Jacob's Well which used to be an altar of worship, revealing to this woman who has come to a natural well how to find the resource of a heavenly well. A study of the encounter between Jesus and this woman reveals some important secrets of the well concerning worship.

Jesus knows that **worship is the only thing that will restore and heal a devastated life**. This woman's life was in a mess; what she needed was not natural resources, but to learn that Jesus is the answer and cure for every malady. However, a problem remains: this woman's concept of worship had been skewed by the deep-seated hatred between the cultures. In order to position her for the power of His presence, He deals with some common fallacies about worship.

Fallacy 1

In John 4:20 the woman said, *"Our fathers worshipped in this mountain; and ye say, that in Jerusalem is the place where men ought to worship."* The most common mistake made about worship is the first thing with which he dealt: **Worship must occur in a certain place**. Most church people believe that worship is something that happens

> **"Anytime an *object* or a *place* eclipses our focus on the *person* of worship it becomes idolatry!"**
>
> Shane Warren

on Sunday mornings, Sunday nights, and Wednesday nights. We have even erected great shrines to mark our **places** of worship. In reality worship transcends **place**; worship has little to do with a **place**, but everything to do with a **person**. To affix worship only to a place is to commit idolatry!

Hezekiah became king at twenty-five years of age. His first act as king was very unusual. He did not erect a monument to his father, nor did he try to improve the economy. His first act as king was to re-establish true worship in Israel. Second Kings 18:1-8 records the following things he did to refocus the people in true worship:

- ☐ He removed high places.
- ☐ He broke the images.
- ☐ He cut down the groves.
- ☐ He broke in pieces the brazen serpent of Moses.

The people at this time were steeped in idol worship. It is interesting that he destroyed some things that were not dedicated to idols, but to the worship of God. For example, he broke in pieces the brazen serpent of Moses. Remember the serpent was fashioned per the instruction of God for the healing of the people of Israel after their having been bitten by serpents (Numbers 21). Why would he destroy such a sacred object? He destroyed it because the people were offering incense to a method or a thing that God had once used. Anytime an **object** or a *place* eclipses our focus on the *person* of worship it becomes idolatry. I was in prayer several years ago concerning a church that I was trying to help that was experiencing a split. The conflict arose because they were renovating the sanctuary to accommodate more growth. A certain group within the church was against the renovation project because it altered their "sacred" sanctuary. In prayer I was rebuking the devil of division for this church when the Lord promptly interrupted me: *"This isn't the work of the Devil; this is Me."* I said, "Lord, I don't understand. How can this be your work?" He replied, *"This group of people has made this **place** more important than me. It must be destroyed or others will be swept into its idolatry. Sometimes I have to pull down and destroy so that I can build."*

Oh, how foolish to attach worship only to a place. One of the greatest lessons about worship ever to be learned is that *worship transcends place.* Worship is spiritual! A true worshipper enjoys the presence of God in his home, at work, or on vacation.

What Does God Want?

Do not misunderstand, this concept is not meant to undermine the power of corporate gatherings in houses of worship; I strongly believe in the power of the local church – I am a pastor! At some point, however, we have to break the mindset that church is a place, a building, and realize that we are the Lord's body--carriers of His presence into every location. This was the message of God to David when the king desired to build God a house—a place. God told David in 2 Samuel 7:4-17, "I never told you to build me a house (paraphrased)...." In verse twenty-seven, God promised David, "...*I will build you a house....*" In essence God was saying to David, "I don't want a *place* in which to dwell. I am looking for a *people* in which to dwell." Jesus quickly states this same principle to the Samaritan woman when he said in John 4:21, *"Woman, believe me, the hour cometh, when ye shall neither in this mountain, nor yet at Jerusalem, worship the father."*

Fallacy 2

The woman follows with another fallacy of worship which is found in John 4:22, *"Ye worship ye know not what; we know what we worship: for salvation is of the Jews."* Jesus knows that this woman's concept of true worship is based on cultural understanding. She has already made the statement that Jews worship one way and that Samaritans worship another; at that time Jesus was dealing with the second fallacy of worship: ***Real worship is based on a certain style***.

> **"Worship is not about the song that you sing, but the heart that you bring!"**
>
> Brad Jackson

How many worship wars are started over the issue of style? What is the most anointed style of worship, Southern Gospel or Contemporary? How many times have I heard statements such as "I wish we had the old red-backed hymnals"; or, "I wish we could put lyrics on a screen." I had just started pastoring when the church first discovered the overhead projector. My parishioners thought I had committed the unpardonable sin when I removed the hymnals and started singing from overheads. How foolish are these frivolous worship wars!

"Worship is not about the song that you sing, but the heart that you bring!" It has been my good fortune to travel the world preaching the Gospel. I have ministered in the remotest parts of Africa where pots, pans, and drums were all that were available to use as musical instruments. Some of the most anointed worship in the world is in those areas. People in those areas are not preoccupied with equipment, lights, or styles. They are preoccupied with Jesus. During my latest trip to Nigeria, I observed worship that was so anointed as hundreds of people manifested demon possession and were delivered through the power of worship. They did not have a hymnal or screens, quality instruments or trained vocalists--just people bringing to God their hearts of worship.

Worship transcends style! When we get to heaven, there will be every style, tribe, tongue, kindred, and nation in full demonstration around the throne. It is foolish to think that everyone will vacate his cultural style and take up the red-backed hymnal. I am sorry if saying these things offends you, but Jesus had to spit in some people's faces to open their eyes. If you are offended, it could be that God is trying to give you a secret from the well of worship. I love Southern Gospel music above all other types. I am convinced that God loves it too, because I like what He likes; however, in my church we do mostly contemporary songs. Why? It is the style that empowers this current generation to worship. Real, biblical worship is the blending of the following styles: psalms, hymns, and spiritual songs (Ephesians 5:19; Colossians 3:16).

Fallacy 3

Finally, there is the last secret from the well--probably the most difficult to receive (John 4:23). *"The hour cometh and now is, when the true **worshippers** shall worship the father in spirit and in truth: for the father **seeketh** such to worship him."* This woman must have been accustomed to worshipping at the temple in Samaria since she knows so much about it. Jesus has shown her that worship is not about a *place* or a *style.* He deals with worship itself. What I am about to say is going to sound sacrilegious, but do not turn a deaf ear--let me explain. Fallacy three is that ***God wants our worship!*** What if I told you that God is not the least bit interested in your worship? Now I have your attention! Jesus deals with the issue of worship itself because people believe that God wants our worship. Here is the truth: ***God is not looking for worship; He is looking for worshippers!*** *Worship* is something that we do, but a *worshipper* is who we are. *Worship* is an act, being a *worshipper* is a lifestyle. Because of believing the third fallacy, many people worship only on certain days, when in reality we should have the heart of worship churning within us continuously (Hebrews 13:15).

The Heart of the Matter

God commands *"...Gather my saints together to me, those who have made a covenant with me by sacrifice."* (Psalm 50:5)   This command sounds like a wonderful thing until you read the context of the passage. God adds in 50:12 these fearful words, *"If I were hungry I would not tell you...."* The context of this passage is that God is upset with His people because they are bringing sacrifices to the temple, but their hearts and lives are not in their acts.   David said in Psalm 51:16, *"For You do not desire sacrifice, or else I would give it; You do not delight in burnt offering."* How can he make such a statement when in Exodus, Leviticus and Deuteronomy, God has commanded that sacrifices be made in certain manners? David can make this bold declaration because worship is not about the sacrifice; it is about the heart.

Worship is a Spirit issue and can be done only in spirit and truth. *God is a Spirit: and they that worship him must worship him in spirit and in truth (John 4:24).*   Real worship is not only an act, but it is a connecting of spirits. God is not at all pleased when we perform the act of worship apart from a life of worship. *"And Samuel said, 'Has the Lord as great delight in burnt offerings and sacrifices, as in obedience to the voice of the Lord? Surely, to obey is better than sacrifice, and to heed than the fat of rams'"* *(1 Samuel 15:22).* The beautiful thing according to the Word is that there are only a few things for which God really looks. One is a worshipper! The Scripture says that God is "seeking such" a person.

I want you to realize that right now God's eyes are running to and fro in the earth looking for someone to whom He can show Himself strong (2 Chronicles 16:9). If a true *worshipper* is what gets the attention of God, would you qualify? If He were looking for someone to bless because at the heart of the issue he is a real worshipper, would He bless you? Are you a true worshipper, or are you someone who just goes through the motions of worship on Sundays or Wednesdays? I do not know about you, but I want God's eyes turned in my direction; as a result I have made up my mind to worship Him with everything within me. When we really understand the power of worship, we will be more diligent to spend time with the Lord. Unfortunately most of us are like the Samaritan woman; we worship, but we do not know what or whom.

In the next chapter, I will show you that the warfare over worship styles is not the real issue. The real issue is that worship is warfare! What if I could show you what happens in the Spirit realm when we worship? What if I told you that Satan, because of his worship ability, knows what happens when we worship? His knowing is the reason he tries so hard to keep you out of the heavenlies. You had better get ready because this book is going to a W.N.L. (Whole Nother Level)!

Chapter 3

The Warfare of Worship

In Exodus 32 is the account of Moses' receiving the commands in the presence of God upon Mt. Sinai. In the valley the people, under the leadership of Aaron, had constructed a golden calf to worship. God is angered by their idol worship and commands Moses to go down the mountain. Half way down Joshua is waiting for Moses and listening to people in the valley below.

When Moses descends to the place where Joshua is waiting, Joshua makes a statement that every believer should study. Exodus 32:15-18 recounts the incident. *"And Moses turned, and went down from the mount, and the two tables of the testimony were in his hand: the tables were written on both their sides; on the one side and on the other were they written. And the tables were the work of God and the writing was the writing of God, graven upon the tables. And when Joshua heard the noise of the people as they shouted, he said unto Moses,*

There is a noise of war in the camp. And he [Moses] said, it is not the voice of them that shout for mastery; neither is it the voice of them that cry for being overcome: but the noise of them that sing do I hear." This passage reveals some incredible keys about worship that will lead us down a path of discovery of its effects on the natural and spiritual realm.

To understand this passage, we must consider its context. The context describes the actions of the people in the valley. What were they doing while Moses was on the mountain? They had built a golden calf and were *worshipping* it. The Hebrew word for *worship* is *shachah. It* means to *bow down* or *prostrate* oneself. The *Jewish Encyclopedia* under *worship* and *gold calf*, reports that the ancient Egyptians would worship this agricultural deity by bowing down and even kissing it in the mouth. The *Septuagint*, the Greek translation of the Hebrew Bible, uses the word *proskuneo* for *worship* which means to *kiss like a dog licking a man's hand.* The following is what was happening down in the valley. The people had built a golden calf. They were running up to it, bowing down in reverence, and licking or kissing it--possibly in the mouth.

Worship Is Warfare

There must have been great music, dancing, shouting, and celebration because verse 17-18 makes it clear that Moses and Joshua could hear the sound coming out of the camp. The **sound of worship is the sound of warfare to the heavenlies!** In Exodus 32:17, Joshua called it the *noise of war*. What were they doing in the valley? They were worshipping! This incident tells me that worship sounds like warfare to the spirit realm. Beloved, if you will seize this principle in your spirit, your life will never be the same. I believe the reason people do not see the value in being true worshippers is that they do not know the power of praise and worship. **Worship is one of the believer's most powerful weapons**.

Notice that Judges 5 records the song of Deborah and Barak in their campaign against Sisera. In the words of this prophetic song, there is an amazing phenomenon.

As Deborah was singing, there was warfare in the heavens. *The stars in their courses* (Judges 5:20), according to the order and direction of the Lord of hosts, *fought against Sisera,* by using malignant influences, or by causing the storms of hail and thunder, which contributed so much to the rout of Sisera's army. The *Chaldee* presents the same situation as *from heaven, from the place where the stars go forth, war was waged against Sisera;* that is, the power of the God of heaven was engaged against him by making use of the ministration of the angels of heaven.

> **"When God's people begin to praise and worship Him using the Biblical methods He gives, the Power of His presence comes among His people in an even greater measure."**
>
> Graham Truscott

In some unique way, the heavenly bodies, although not arrested, as when the sun stood still at Joshua's word, but going on in their courses, fought against Sisera.

Those who oppose the God of heaven are enemies with whom the whole creation is at war. Perhaps the flashes of lightning by which the stars fought was what frightened the horses, so much that they pranced until their very hoofs were broken (Judges 5:22), and probably overturned the chariots of iron which they drew or turned them back upon their owners. Then the river of Kishon, which also fought against their enemies, was released and swept away multitudes of those who had hoped to make their escape through it (Judges 5:21). In this passage there is a powerful revelation of worship. As Deborah prophetically worshipped, war in the heavenlies erupted which accomplished the victory in the war upon the earth. Friend, **worship is warfare**!

Again, there is a pattern throughout the Word of God's putting worshippers in front of armies as they go into battle. When the Moabites, the Ammonites, and the Edomites invaded Judah, Jehoshaphat, the king, was facing the battle of his life. As a result he sought the Lord's will through prayer. God responded to him through Jahaziel, *"Don't be afraid of this multitude. The battle is not yours but Mine. You won't need to fight, but you will see the victory"* (2 Chronicles 15-17).   Upon hearing this assurance, the Levites praised the Lord *"with a loud voice on high"* (v. 19).   How were the people of Judah able to win this war without fighting?   In what seems to us a highly unusual tactic, Jehoshaphat put the choir out in front of the army (2 Chronicles 20:21).   The choir began to praise the Lord in anticipation of the truth of His word.   As they did so, the enemy was defeated (v. 22).   The praise of Jehoshaphat's choir must have been quite different from most of our worship and praise. Much praise today sounds as if we are more influenced by the enemy than by a triumphant ring of victory.   *"Let the high praises of God be in their mouth, and a two-edged sword in their hand"* (Ps. 149:6).   When Jehoshaphat and his choir went out to praise God, they won the victory. Praise and worship changes things because it reminds us to trust the One who can give us victory when we are armed only with songs and instruments.   The scripture is clear that the **warfare is won through the weapon of worship**. There is not a war you currently face that cannot be won with the weapon of worship.

Since we know warfare is connected to worship, look at one more truth from a passage found in Exodus 32:18, *"and he [Moses] said, it is not the voice of them that shout for mastery, neither is it the voice of them that cry for being overcome: but the noise of them that sing do I hear."* Moses stopped to listen to the noise of warfare coming from the camp. As he listened to the praise of the people, he recognized that it was not people's shouting because they had won the victory, nor was it the cry of help for victory; rather, it was simply the sound of people's singing. Paul describes such singing in 1 Corinthians 13:1, as *"...sounding brass and tinkling cymbals...."* I wonder how many times the great God of heaven listens to our worship services only to find a group of people who are making a sound while going through only the act and motions of worship. They are not true worshippers who understand the spiritual dynamics of worship, but people who are performing the act of worship without the heart of worship. How many times have you gone to church and walked through the motions without your heart's ever engaging heaven? You might ask, "Why are the spiritual dynamics of worship so important?"

First Corinthians 11:10 seems to be warning us that angels attend our worship services. It says, *"That is why a woman ought to have a veil on her head, **because of the angels"** (*RSV). In Corinthians Paul is dealing with the context of corporate worship. He seems to be indicating that we need to be careful how we approach worship. Specifically in this passage he is dealing with the local custom of women's covering their heads because there are angels present. According to Hebrews 1:14, angels are *"ministering spirits sent forth to minister for them who shall be heirs of salvation."* Angels are employed throughout the Word of God on man's behalf; they are also active in the ministry of Jesus and in the New Testament church. Consequently, it would only stand to reason that angels are still very active in the lives of believers and in God's church today. If such be the case, angels are present in our worship services for various ministries. At the same time, we know there are fallen angels as well. These fallen angels are on assignment against the will of God in the earth and in our lives. This truth is made very evident through the experience of Daniel (Daniel 10:12-13).

Do you realize the power of what I have just taught you? Angels, fallen and good, are attending our worship services. I believe that when we gather for worship, corporately or personally, that there is a sound of warfare that is released in the heavens. At that point the angels assemble by the instruction of the Holy Spirit to do business in our lives. The question at hand is when they arrive, do they find real worshippers releasing a sound of warfare, or just simply find people going through the motions of worship?

Recently, in one of our services at the church where I am pastor, we had a powerful outpouring of God's manifested presence during an intense time of prophetically-charged worship. The atmosphere was saturated like electricity with the glory of God. Believers could physically feel the power of God. During this time a young man who was totally blind instantaneously received his sight before almost a thousand people. I, along with the rest of the congregation, was awestruck as we watched this young man that we all knew well see for the first time. I will never forget when my usher brought me the news that the *blind man* could see. His precious young wife wept as she watched her husband read signs, count fingers, and point out colors. Imagine what happened to my church's growth after that miracle occurred!

Something strange had happened the night before that service. I awoke out of a deep sleep, sat up, and heard these words: *"Angels will be at church tomorrow!"* I jumped from the bed and immediately went into a time of prayer seeking God's direction for the day of worship. My heart was drawn to the story of Joshua and the walls of Jericho. I noticed something that I had never seen before: when Joshua arrived at the walls of the city, the angel of the Lord was already there. All of a sudden out of my spirit man came rushing these words: *"Angels will be at church tomorrow! Tell the people all they have to do is show up with a shout!"* When the presence and power of God became tangible in the service the next day, I stood and declared to the people what I felt that the Lord had said. Immediately the place erupted with a roar that sounded like a thousand lions; miracles started happening all over the building.

God wants me to tell you that **worship is warfare**, that when you worship there is a sound released in the heavens to which angels respond. All you have to do is **show up with a shout!** What if I told you that angels were not the only heavenly beings coming to our worship services? What if I could show you that there are others who are coming to our worship services? What if Jesus were to attend one of your church services?   In the following chapters, I am going to prove to you that He does. I will then show you what He does when He gets there. Remember, the Lord is looking for *worshippers*, not worship! I wonder what the Lord does when He finds a true *worshipper.*

Chapter 4

What Satan Knows About Worship

I have found the Bible to be an amazing book! Just when I think I have seen everything and learned every principle, God reveals a new facet of His glory to me. Paul calls this the *manifold* wisdom of God. God's knowledge and wisdom is *eternal* and *manifold*. Just when I think I have reached the apex of revelation knowledge, He rolls back another pleat for discovery. The scripture has layers of revelation; it is equally profound to the learned student, as well as to the novice. Because it has layers of revelation, our discovery of God is an eternal process. Imagine spending an eternity discovering the different facets of His unfathomable wisdom.

Woven within the fabric of Ezekiel 28 is one of those revelatory pleats. It is a curious chapter in the Bible. Verses one through nineteen seem to present two different persons, the Prince of Tyre (1-10) and the King of Tyre (vs. 11-19). These two kings received two different declarations. The first was of judgment, and the second was of lamentation. It is very evident that both of these kings were guilty of the sin of pride. Both possessed great wisdom and wealth; however, they abused their privileges and thus offended the God of heaven. Many theologians believe that the Prince of Tyre mentioned in verses 1-10 was a ruler of the city when Nebuchadnezzar invaded, but they see the King of Tyre as Satan, the enemy of God and of the Jewish people. I believe that the King of Tyre, Satan himself, energized the Prince of Tyre, an earthly ruler, and used him to accomplish Satan's own personal purposes. This pattern is also in the book of Daniel and Revelation where the Anti-Christ, an earthly ruler, is energized by Satan to accomplish his wicked agenda during the tribulation period. The Prince is called a *man* in Ezekiel 28:2, but the king is called the *anointed cherub* in 28:14.

The verses that speak of the King of Tyre give the impression that this king is much more than a human regent, but that he is Satan himself. First Chronicles 21, Daniel 9, and Matthew 4:8-10 make it abundantly clear that Satan wants to control the nations and their leaders. The very use of the word *cherub* in Ezekiel 28:4 shows that he is an angelic creature. Another clue to the subject of these verses is found in 28:14. This angelic creature is positioned in the Garden of Eden and in the holy mountain of God. This passage sounds much like the one found in Isaiah 14:12; therefore, I believe that Ezekiel 28:11-19 is a prophetic passage about Satan, his **original** role in the **earth,** and his fall due to rebellion and pride.

Satan's Original Role

Satan began as an obedient angel, but rebelled against God and led a revolt to steal God's throne. The text describes him in his pre-fall state as a beautiful angel whose body was covered with nine jewels mounted in the finest of gold. The jewels are also found on the breastplate of the Jewish High Priest (Exodus 28:17-20). In addition his position in the Garden of Eden and upon God's holy mountain shows that this angel had special priestly functions to perform for the Lord. Interestingly, believers have been empowered with the nine gifts of the

Holy Spirit and nine fruit of the Spirit. I believe that these nine gifts help to perform the priestly function before the Lord and that the nine fruit of the Spirit gives the character of God for the Christian walk. Satan had nine gifts, the stones, but he was not equipped with the character of God, hence, his fall.

According to Ezekiel 28:13 and Isaiah 14:11, the angel Lucifer also had special musical abilities. Verse 28:13 records that he had percussion instruments and woodwinds created within his body; Isaiah 14:11 states that he had viols, stringed instruments, as well. Evidently, Lucifer functioned as some kind of worshiping instrument or possibly the leader of worship in the Garden of Eden. With all of the world's perverted music and lyrics, one must wonder, "Is Satan still playing in his rebellious state? Could it be that the world's music is only emulating the wicked sound from the fallen angel?"

One final clue to this angel and his operation is in Ezekiel 28:14. The Bible calls him the "anointed cherub that covereth...." This phrase is an old English idiom that means that he was an angel that had a specific assignment of authority over something. The question is what did he control?" The answer is found in several passages. First, in Ezekiel 28:13-14 it is clear that he is upon the earth for he is in the Garden of Eden. When Ezekiel 28:14 says that he was upon "the holy mountain of God," it does not mean heaven. It seems that Isaiah 14 confirms this conclusion. Isaiah 14:11-15 gives the story of Satan's rebellion and fall from authority. In verses 13 and 14, Satan is *ascending into heaven* to try to dethrone God. If he were already in heaven, why would he need to *ascend* there? Scripture indicates that there are three heavens (2 Corinthians 12:12): earth's atmosphere, outer space, and the heaven in which God dwells. Isaiah 14:14 states that Satan is trying to ascend "above the heights of the clouds." The clouds are in the first heaven or earth's atmosphere. The implication is that Satan was an angel who was assigned at one time authority over the earth. It is clear that he tried to lead a rebellion to overthrow God and that one-third of the angels joined him in the mutiny.

He was no ordinary angel. He was an angelic creature of unusual beauty with a fascinating priestly worship assignment. Lucifer's original role and responsibility before his rebellion is clear. He performed priestly function; he was an anointed cherub that *covered* the earth; he was a worship instrument or leader of worship; he was created with three of four classes of instruments needed to make perfect music--percussion, woodwinds, strings, and brass.

Understanding this revelation, the Christian knows why Satan fights worship as he does! Satan has a first-hand, eyewitness account of the effect of worship upon God and the angels. Furthermore, when Satan led his revolt and was defeated, he lost his position of authority over the *earth*. God then made man, put him in the same Garden of Eden and gave him dominion and authority. For all intents and purposes, believers are Satan's replacement. Through vocal chords, hands, fingers, and feet worshipers have abilities to produce music and express worship to the Father. Beloved, get this fact in your heart! The reason Satan fights throughout Scripture for the earth, for nations, and against the church is that he used to have authority over the earth as God's most beautifully created angel. His authority was attached to his worship abilities.

One of the greatest warfare tools is the weapon of worship. Nothing moves the heavens like worship! Satan has seen the effect of worship upon the heavens and the Godhead. There is something so powerful about worship that he does not want the body of Christ to discover. To pervert worship, Satan constantly attempts to draw men away from true worship to go whoring after other gods. Worship is at the heart of every issue of humanity. Man was created to worship; therefore, he will worship something! It might be success, spouses, dreams, or destination; but, he will worship something because that is the way he has been created. Why does Satan constantly fight to keep men from discovering the power of worship? He knows that true worship is the *pathway to dominion* for the Christian.

Chapter 5

The Pathway to Dominion

If Satan were created as a worshipping angel and were given authority over the earth, then worship must be a key to spiritual dominion. In Genesis 1:26 and 28, God said, *"...Let us make man in our image, after our likeness: and let them have dominion over the fish of the sea, and over the fowl of the air, and over the cattle, and over all the earth, and over every creeping thing that creepeth upon the earth... And God blessed them, and God said unto them, Be fruitful, and multiply, and replenish the earth, and subdue it: and have dominion over the fish of the sea, and over the fowl of the air, and over every living thing that moveth upon the earth."*

> **"Worship changes the worshiper into the image of the One worshiped"**
> Jack Hayford

When God created the heavens and the earth, He always used a source for His creation. For example, when God wanted plants, He spoke to the dirt. When

51

God wanted birds, He spoke to the air. When God wanted animals, He spoke to the ground. When God wanted fish, He spoke to the water. As Myles Monroe said on page 21 of his book *Understanding Your Potential*, "All things have the same source components and essence as their source. What God created is, in essence, like the substance from which it came." When He came to the creation of man, the same creative formula applied; however, this time God did not speak to the dirt, air, or water. When He created man, God spoke directly to *Himself*. God created man by speaking to Himself! In the beginning God took something from Himself and put it into Adam so that Adam would be like Him and share in His life.

Once God created Adam and placed him in the Garden, He gave Adam legal dominion over the earth. Although Satan had once been the "anointed cherub" that covered the earth, now because of his rebellion God took that glorious position from him and gave it to man whom He anointed to rule the earth just as Satan once had ruled. Psalm 82:6 declares, *"I have said, Ye are gods; and all of you are children of the most High."* The Lord made mankind, beginning with Adam and Eve, to be the *gods* of this world. The previous statement needs some clarification: Adam and Eve were not *Gods* in the sense of Divinity, but they were made to be *gods* in the sense of authority or dominion. The Bible is very plain. Deuteronomy 6:4 declares His name is Jehovah, and He has only one begotten son Jesus Christ. On the other hand, in God's creative order, He put man in authority and expected him to dominate the earth. Based on the description given in Genesis 2:8, at the time of the creation of Adam and Eve, the Garden of Eden did not cover the entire earth. *"And the Lord God planted a garden eastward in Eden; and there he put the man whom he had formed."* God gave man the responsibility to tend the garden, dominate it, and multiply it until it covered the earth. Based on God's eternal plan, this all-encompassing garden will one day be realized when God creates a New Heaven and a New Earth.

Psalm 115:16 says, *"The heaven, even the heavens, are the Lord's: but the earth hath he given to the children of men."* God literally gave the earth to mankind. The great Creator of the heavens and the earth gave man the power and authority to rule over the earth. Unfortunately, Satan, having once ruled over the earth, saw a great opportunity to regain ownership. He saw the unconditional authority delegated to man. Then he tempted mankind to yield that authority by directly disobeying God's commands. When Adam and Eve disobeyed God, a transfer of dominion, not ownership because the earth belongs to the Lord, was given into the hands of Satan. At that point Satan became *"... the **god of this world**" who "has blinded the minds of the unbelieving so that they might not see the light of the gospel of the glory of Christ, who is the image of God (2 Corinthians 4:4)."* Mankind lost control from that point forward as death entered the world through one man's disobedience; however, God sent His son Jesus Christ to the earth as a man to restore man's dominion.

Reclaiming Our Authority

For thirty-three years Jesus walked this earth totally yielded to the Holy Spirit and submitted to God the Father. Not once did He capitulate to temptation and relinquish His heavenly position. *For we have not an high* *priest which cannot be touched with the feeling of our infirmities; but was in all points tempted like as we are, **yet without sin"** (Hebrew 5:14).* By virtue of the atoning work of the cross, Jesus, through obedience unto death (*Philippians 2:8*), reclaimed and restored man's legal right to dominion. Some of our Lord's final words are *"And Jesus came and spake unto them, saying, **All power is given unto me in heaven and in earth**. Go ye therefore, and teach all nations, baptizing them in the name of the Father, and of the Son, and of the Holy Ghost: Teaching them to observe all things whatsoever I have commanded you: and, lo, I am with you alway, even unto the end of the world. Amen."* The *"Go ye…"* implies that the dominion and authority that our Lord had has been transferred unto every believer in Jesus Christ. Now, because of the Lord's redemptive work, every believer has been *"…made alive together with Christ (by grace you have been saved), and raised us up with Him, and seated us with Him in the heavenly places in Christ Jesus…" (Ephesians 2:5-6).* All Christians have been raised up and seated with Christ, yet are all still here upon the earth. Believers' physical position did not change, but their spiritual position did! All now in Him are seated *"Far above all rule and authority and power and dominion and every name that is named [above every title that can be conferred], not only in this age and in this world, but also in the age and the world which are to come"* (Ephesians 1:21).

What does the believer's spiritual position have to do with the subject of worship? If Satan were created as a worshipping angel to have dominion over this earth, if Christians are his replacement, then worship has everything to do with it! Worship was Satan's pathway to dominion as well as his pathway out of dominion. Beloved, worship is also every believer's pathway in and out of dominion. When man ceased to worship God through obedience, he lost his authority; on the other hand, when Jesus, the God-man, worshiped God through total obedience, He regained authority for man!

> **"We must learn to *work* out of rest and *warfare* out of worship!"**
>
> *Bill Johnson*

Genesis 49:8-10 says, *"Judah, thou art he whom thy brethren shall praise: thy hand shall be in the neck of thine enemies; thy father's children shall bow down before thee. Judah is a lion's whelp: from the prey, my son, thou art gone up: he stooped down, he couched as a lion, and as an old lion; who shall rouse him up? The scepter shall not depart from Judah, nor a lawgiver from between his feet, until Shiloh come; and unto him shall the gathering of the people be."* This passage is rich with truth that connects worship with spiritual authority. The name *Judah* means *praise*. When one reads this passage and inserts the word *praise* for *Judah,* the authority factor of worship becomes easily apparent. For example, verse ten declares that the *scepter shall not depart from Judah.* *Wikipedia* states that the scepter was an ornamented staff or rod that has long represented **authority**. Translated properly, this verse declares "**Authority** *shall not depart from* **praise**...." Verse eight states that Judah's *"hand shall be in the neck of thine enemies...."* Again, there is the authority factor of worship. Translated accurately it says, *"***Praise***...thy hand shall be in the neck of thine enemies...."* Believers must understand what this statement means. **Praise can choke out any enemy that Satan uses!**

This same principle occurs in Judges 20:18, *"And the children of Israel arose, and went up to the house of God, and asked counsel of God, and said, Which of us shall go up first to the battle against the children of Benjamin? And the LORD said, Judah shall go up first."* Notice, Judah—praise—goes into battle first. Worship is a weapon of warfare that must go first! Until the believer grasps this revelation, he will be overwhelmed with oppression and Satanic activity. The pathway to dominion and authority is through the warfare of worship. One day while I was in the throes of one of my worst personal struggles, I was listening to a podcast by Bill Johnson, one of my favorite communicators and a pastor in Redding, California. He made a statement that confirmed what God was saying in me at that time about worship: "We must learn to *work* out of rest and *warfare* out of worship!" Beloved, this is a powerful spiritual principle! Worship chokes the enemy to death; it is one of the primary scepters of authority given to the believer.

Satan hates worship! He knows what it does to the heavens, how it affects God and the worshipper, and even how it affects him. Slewfoot understands that revelation and application of worship are spiritual weapons with which he cannot reckon. I hope, by now, that every believer is starting to connect the dots concerning why worship is so significant, its affect in the spirit realm, and the authority it creates in the life of the believer!

Chapter 6

Betrayed by a Kiss

Chapter three emphasizes that the word *worship* in Hebrew is *shachah* which means to *bow down* or *prostrate* oneself. The *Jewish Encyclopedia* under *worship* and *gold calf* reports that the ancient Egyptians would worship this agricultural deity by bowing down and possibly kissing it in the mouth. The *Septuagint,* the Greek translation of the Hebrew Bible, uses the word *proskuneo* for *worship* which means to *kiss like a dog licking a man's hand.* Worship is a very intimate act and should be taken very seriously!

Matthew 26:47-50 reports this terrible incident, *"And while he yet spake, lo, Judas, one of the twelve, came, and with him a great multitude with swords and staves, from the chief priests and elders of the people. Now he that betrayed him gave them a sign, saying, Whomsoever I shall **kiss**, that same is he: hold him fast. And forthwith he came to Jesus, and said, Hail, master;*

and kissed him. And Jesus said unto him, Friend, wherefore art thou come? Then came they, and laid hands on Jesus, and took him." This sad account of our Lord's betrayal at the hands of Judas Iscariot teaches one of the most powerful worship principles yet. Judas, thinking that Jesus would be hard to find and that the disciples would put up a fight, brought a band of soldiers, armed and carrying lanterns, to arrest the Lord. Judas' actions prove that he did not really understand Jesus. Even more tragic is the fact that Judas betrayed Jesus with a *kiss*; an act that was not necessary since Jesus clearly told the soldiers who He was.

"Hail, master" was a usual compliment among the Jews. Judas pretends to wish our Lord continued health while he is meditating his destruction! How many compliments of this kind are there in the world! Judas had a pattern in Joab (2 Samuel 20:9-10), who, while he pretends by a kiss to inquire tenderly for the health of Amasa, thrusts him through with his sword. The disciple Judas vastly outdoes his pattern Joab, and through a motive, if possible, still more base. Let all those who use

unmeaning or insidious compliments rank forever with Joab and Judas.

Judas' name means *praise*. Judas, a worshipper betrayed the Lord with the *kiss of worship*. He used the *kiss* as a weapon against the Lord instead of the enemy Satan. To make matters worse, the Greek verb indicates that Judas *kissed* Jesus *repeatedly*; he did not kiss Jesus just once, but multiple times. In that day it was customary for disciples to kiss their teacher in respect and honor, but this kiss was not the kiss of honor or worship; it was the kiss of betrayal! How it must have crushed the Lord's heart to be betrayed by the thing that He loves the most, *the kiss of worship*! Judas fulfilled the words of Matthew 15:8, *"These people draw near to Me with their mouth, And honor Me with their lips, But their heart is far from Me."*

The lips of Judas were not common lips. As Paul Harvey so perfectly says, "Now here's the rest of the story." John 12:1-6 records Judas' attitude about a woman's extravagant worship of Jesus: *"Then Jesus six days* before the passover came to Bethany, where Lazarus was which had been dead, whom he raised from the dead. There they made him a supper; and Martha served: but Lazarus was one of them that sat at the table with him. Then took Mary a pound of ointment of spikenard, very costly, and anointed the feet of Jesus, and wiped his feet with her hair: and the house was filled with the odour of the ointment. Then saith one of his disciples, Judas Iscariot, Simon's son, which should betray him, Why was not this ointment sold for three hundred pence, and given to the poor? This he said, not that he cared for the poor; but because he was a thief, and had the bag, and bare what was put therein." A woman named Mary is worshipping the Lord with very costly

> **"Without worship, we go about miserable."**
>
> A.W. Tozer

ointment. This account is also found in Matthew 26:6-13 and Mark 14:3-9. The combination of all three accounts makes it clear that Mary used a great amount of very costly oil because she anointed His head and His feet. It was an act of pure love and worship on her part. She had a prophetic sense that something was coming soon in the way of suffering for Jesus. It would have required a year's wages from a common laborer to purchase that ointment. Like David, Mary had determined not to give the Lord that which cost her nothing (2 Samuel 24:24). This powerful act of worship changed the atmosphere of the house with its fragrance and became a story that has been spread around the world (Matthew 26:13). It was Judas who criticized this beautiful act of worship and fueled the comments of the other disciples. Judas, however, was a devil (John 12:70); and John must have seen through his façade of religious activity.

John 12:4 records the first words uttered by Judas; Matthew 27:4 records his final words. In both passages it is clear that Judas was a thief and was in the habit of stealing money from the money-bag that he carried. The Greek word for bag found in John 12:6 is *glossokomon* which originally meant a small case in which mouthpieces for wind instruments were kept. For me, this is the most profound part of this story: the only person in Israel who carried that kind of bag was a *musician*. At one time Judas was a player of wind instruments. Possibly Jesus chose him for his worship ability. As stated before, Judas' name means *praise,* and he is carrying a *musician's* bag, gig bag. At this point Judas is not only stealing money but he is also *merchandising his anointing* and betraying the Lord with the very thing that he was created to do! Ezekiel 28 records the activity of Satan and the reason for his fall. Verse 16 of Chapter 28 says that Satan, in his pride, *merchandised* his anointing. This anointed cherub that God created to rule by worship betrayed the Lord my using his gift for his own personal gain.

Merchandising The Anointing

At this point I must now speak to preachers and worshippers, those in full-time Christian service. I am very concerned about the *merchandising* of preaching and worship in the body of Christ. I believe in people's having products available that help strengthen others' walks with Christ, and I also understand that ministries have budgets and need necessary finances for operation. On the other hand, I believe that it dishonors God for preachers and worshippers to take what they have been created to do and *merchandise,* promote it for sale. Our gifts and talents are not for sale! Yes, the Lord provides for those of us in full-time ministry through our gifts and talents; but if we allow pride and the lust for money to move us to a place of commercializing our anointing, we sin the great sin of betrayal!

I am amazed at the groups and preachers who have set prices on their ministries. Recently, our church hosted two internationally-known guests. One had a set price, and the other required nothing more than expenses and a love offering by faith. The one who set a price received his required thirty-five hundred dollars; however, the one who came by faith left with over fifteen thousand dollars. What was the difference? The difference was the anointing of the Holy Ghost upon ministry! It strikes me strange that these ministries who require tens of thousands of dollars to minister will come and preach a faith to our people that they themselves do not have. Sometimes I wonder if some preachers and singers have ever read what the Bible states in Mark 6:7-11, "*And He called to Him the Twelve [apostles] and began to send them out [as His ambassadors] two by two and gave them authority and power over the unclean spirits.*" **He**

charged them to take nothing for their journey except a walking stick--no bread, no wallet for a collection bag, no money in their belts which are girdles or purses-- *"But to go with sandals on their feet and not to put on two tunics [undergarments]. And He told them, wherever you go into a house, stay there until you leave that place. And if any community will not receive and accept and welcome you, and they refuse to listen to you, when you depart, shake off the dust that is on your feet, for a*

> **"As worship begins in holy expectancy, it ends in holy obedience. Holy obedience saves worship from becoming an opiate, an escape from the pressing needs of modern life."**
>
> Richard Foster

testimony against them. Truly I tell you, it will be more tolerable for Sodom and Gomorrah in the judgment day than for that town." If they were not supposed to take money, then it means that they had to trust God to provide for their ministry. Has it dawned on anyone else that maybe these ministries that require so much money-guaranteed-up-front do not have a substantial faith revelation or anointing to move people to respond through giving? If that be the case, why do we continue this madness of *merchandising* the anointing in the church world? Just a thought!

Before we get too carried away, let us make this passage a little more personal in application. Judas, the musician and praiser, betrayed Jesus with the kiss of worship by honoring Him with his lips and dishonoring Him with his heart. How many times have you and I come to worship services and have gone through the motions of worship, yet did not really enter in with our hearts? Are we not guilty of Judas' sin? Are we not honoring God with our lips of worship without our hearts being engaged? Unfortunately, this describes many of our common church experiences! If you have failed in this area, I encourage you to do as I have done. Repent and ask the Lord to forgive you for betraying Him with the thing He created you to do and with what He enjoys most-- worship.

Chapter 7

Jesus Sings and God Dances

Worship is a spiritual affair! Jesus said, *"God is a Spirit: and they that worship Him must worship Him in spirit and in truth (John 4:24)."* There is no such thing as true worship without the spirit engaged! Since God is Spirit, it follows logically that the worship brought to Him must be essentially of a spiritual kind. The key word in this verse is *must*: Jesus is not speaking of just a desirable element of true worship; rather, He is insistent that this is the *essential* element of true worship. Paul speaks of this kind of intimacy with God in Romans 1:9, *"For God is my witness, whom I serve with my spirit in the gospel of his Son...."* In John 4 the context of this teaching on worship is centered upon the subject of life-giving water. In the context of this passage, it is highly probable that Jesus is alluding to true spiritual worship's being "connected to the life-giving activity of God" (*The New International Commentary* pg. 272). So many believers miss this wonderful benefit of true Spirit-inspired worship which is tapping into the life-giving activity of God through the medium of worship.

The Samaritans worshipped in ignorance (John 4:22), as do so many in the body of Christ today, because they did not understand the *spirit* of worship. The Jewish Rabbis charged the Samaritans with *superstitious* worship because their worship did not originate from "love and knowledge, but ignorance and fear" (*Daily Study Bible*, Gospel of John I, p. 159). On the contrary, genuine worship occurs when the spirit, the immortal and invisible part of man, speaks to and meets with God. It is the spirit of a man, through worship, which attains to friendship and intimacy with God. We must understand the spiritual dynamics of true Spirit-led worship because all other worship activities are nothing more than religious calisthenics. I am not interested in useless religious activity that appeals only to the carnal nature; rather, I desire to worship and to find the life-giving waters of the Spirit realm as I worship. "All utterances and forms of worship derive their value and their power from their being the manifestation of spiritual life and spiritual aspirations" (Charles Spurgeon).

Since true worship is essentially spiritual, we must now discover the Spirit realm and the effects of worship upon it. What really transpires during our worship, personally and corporately? Hebrews 2:11-12 is a fascinating passage about what actually occurs in worship services. It says, *"For both he that sanctifieth and they who are sanctified are all of one: for which cause he is not ashamed to call them brethren, Saying, I will declare thy name unto my brethren, in the midst of the church will I sing praise unto thee."* The first part of this verse reveals the powerful position of believers and Jesus' attitude toward them. He is not ashamed to call us His brethren. He also considers Himself and believers one! Think of that! We are brothers and sisters with Jesus Christ! When He says that we are *"all of one,"* He is saying the same thing as Romans 8:17, *"And if children, then **heirs**; **heirs** of God, and **joint-heirs** with Christ; if so be that we suffer with him, that we may be also glorified together."* Whatever God will do for Jesus, He will do for us. Hallelujah! That statement is followed with another profound declaration concerning Jesus' activity in our worship services.

Look Who's Talking!

Hebrews 2:12 states that Jesus attends church, and it also tells what He does when He arrives. Matthew 18:20 says, *"For where two or three are gathered together in my name, there am I in the midst of them."* Psalm 22:3 reminds us that God is enthroned upon the praises of His people. Simply put, when believers come together in a worship setting, there is a host of spiritual activity occurring. First Corinthians 11 declares clearly that angels are visiting our services for ministry purposes. Hebrews 2:11-12 in conjunction with Matthew 18 and Psalm 22 informs us that Jesus in present in our worship services as well. According to the passage in Hebrews 2, Jesus is doing specific things in our services: declaring the names of God to His brethren and even joining the congregation in singing worship to the Father.

Hebrews 2:12 first says, "*... I will declare thy name unto my brethren....*" The important thing to note here is that Jesus is the one doing the speaking! When God revealed His name to Moses it was *Yahweh: "And God said to Moses, "I AM Who I AM... This is my name forever, the* *name by which I am to be remembered from generation to generation"* (Ex. 3:14-15). Until that time the children of Israel, including Abraham, Isaac, and Jacob, had not known God as *Jehovah*, but by the name of *God Almighty* (Exodus 6:3). At this time, God began to reveal to His people the full meaning of His redemptive name. *Jehovah* means the *self-existent one* or *eternal one who reveals Himself.* The Lord instructed Moses that Jehovah is His name forever. It was to be a memorial to remind Israel that God's word of promise, God's covenant with them, was forever. He is eternal and unchangeable and, therefore, faithful and unchangeable in His word and promises as well as in His nature. However, as different needs arose among the children of Israel during their history, the Lord revealed Himself as the one who could meet those needs. There is only one God Jehovah; but God has a plethora of attributes that He wants to reveal to mankind. He wants His people to know that He is not just a supreme being suspended in a place called heaven. In all of His sovereignty, He wants to be intimately involved in the lives of His people. The redemptive names of God reveal His redemptive relationship to believers.

In the Old Testament, there are seven redemptive names of the Lord that demonstrate He is capable of meeting every area of human need. Jehovah's seven names are as followers:

- *Jehovah Jireh - The Lord our Provision*
- *Jehovah Rapha – The Lord our Healer*
- *Jehovah Nissi – The Lord our Banner*
- *Jehovah Shalom – The Lord our Peace*
- *Jehovah Rohi – The Lord our Shepherd*
- *Jehovah Tsidkenu – The Lord our Righteousness*
- *Jehovah Shammah – The Lord is Here*

According to Hebrew 2, Jesus is present in our worship services as we are building a seat for Him through praise. When two or more have gathered, He is there in the midst. John 4:23 states that when He arrives, He is *seeking* for the true worshippers. When a true worshipper is found, He then goes to that individual and declares the redemptive names of God in his spiritual ear. For example, suppose there are people in the service who need financial miracles; Jesus walks up to them and says, "I am *Jehovah Jireh–your provider*!"

Some who are attending need divine healing; the Lord walks over to them and says, "I am *Jehovah Rapha–your healer*!" Maybe there is a single mom in the room whose life has been shattered by divorce and who does not know which way to turn; Jesus walks up to her and says, "I am *Jehovah Shalom–your peace*."

Have you ever noticed that there are times in your worship when you feel a change in your spirit? The circumstances might not have changed, but you feel encouraged in spite of contrary issues. I believe with all my heart that what I am teaching you is what is happening. In our congregation we have witnessed numerous miracles: blinded eyes opened, deaf ears healed, cancerous tumors dissolved, *etc.* In every instance the miracles have come during times of heavy worship. I believe that at that moment Jesus walked into the room and started whispering the

> **"The most valuable thing the Psalms do for me is to express the same delight in God which made David dance."**
>
> *C.S. Lewis*

redemptive names of God in the ears of the people based on their needs!

As Jesus is declaring the names of God to the brethren, at some point He seems to be caught up in worship and begins to sing with the church to the Father. Notice Hebrews 2:12, *"...in the midst of the church will I sing praise unto thee."* Again, this is Jesus speaking! In the midst of the church, Jesus starts singing praises to God the Father with the congregation. It is one thing for me, a fallible, weak human being to be worshipping the Father; but it is another thing altogether different when Jesus starts singing to the Father! What an awesome thought that the Son of God is in the church singing with the people. Let me ask you a pointed question that I ask myself almost every service, "If Jesus were in our service would He enjoy our worship?" More than just our singing is happening during worship. Angels are active, and the Son of God is in our midst!

Let us look at what God the Father in heaven is doing while Jesus and the angels are active in our church services. Zephaniah 3:17 says, *"The LORD thy God in the midst of thee is mighty; he will save, he will rejoice over thee with joy; he will rest in his love, he will joy over thee with singing."* This passage is loaded with revelation about heavenly activity! It states that God *"in our midst"* is mighty. To attract the Lord into our midst, Psalm says that we must build Him a chair through praise and worship. Once He inhabits our praise God then *"...rejoices over thee with joy."* The word *rejoice* means *to be joyful, be happy, be delighted, be elated, be ecstatic, be overjoyed, be jubilant, be rapturous, jump for joy, be on cloud nine, be in seventh heaven; celebrate, cheer.*

Get this picture in your mind: God, cheering and jumping in the heavens and being filled with joy and happiness concerning us. Then Zephaniah says, *"He will rest in His love...."* It is as if God becomes excited when we start worshipping, and then He calms Himself for a moment. Next the Bible makes a beautiful declaration, *"He will joy over thee with singing."* The word *joy* here can mean *to twirl and dance with great and happy emotion.* Think about it. As we are singing to God, He is dancing in the heavens and singing back to us!

When we tie all of this together, we get a wonderful picture of what is happening during worship in the Spirit realm. As we are worshipping according to 1 Corinthians 11, angels come into the service for ministry purposes. Jesus is enthroned upon our praises and actually, according to Hebrews 2:11-12, begins to walk in the midst of the congregation declaring the names of God to the brethren. At some point, Jesus then turns and joins in unison with the church in singing praises unto the Father. In the heavens God the Father is rejoicing from the throne, jumping and leaping with great joy and dancing over us, His children, as He is singing a love song back to us.

I was always taught that Jesus and God do not like dancing, but I have since learned that They are not nearly so religious as we are. In fact, Jesus is the express image of the Father! In Luke 10 Jesus commissioned His disciples for ministry and sent them out in His power. When they returned, they were all rejoicing over their ministerial results and the powerful manifestations that they had experienced. In Luke 10:21 the Bible says that Jesus *"...rejoiced in spirit...."* Again, the word *rejoice* means *to exult, dance, celebrate, etc.* In Luke 15 there is a hint of God's love for His children and of the celebration that occurs as a result of salvation. I have always been taught, as have most of you, that when a sinner gets saved that all of the angels rejoice in heaven. I have since learned that I was taught wrongly. Luke 15:10 says, *"Likewise, I say unto you, there is **joy in the presence of the angels of God** over one sinner that repenteth."* Notice, it does not say that the angels rejoice; it says that there is joy in the presence of the angels. I believe God and Jesus are celebrating in the heavens. I have learned that both God and Jesus like to sing and dance.

One final thought along these lines is that when God dances He is standing up from His throne. According to my best study, I can find only three things that make God arise from His throne: martyrdom, worship, and a salvation. In Acts when Stephen was martyred at the hands of Saul, later known as Paul, Jesus stood up at the right hand of God. Psalm 68:1 says, *"Let God arise and his enemies be scattered...."* Accordingly, all through the book of Psalms there is the thought of God's arising and enemies being defeated. So, if worship makes God arise from His throne and if His enemies are scattered when He arises, then worship is a major key to victorious Christian living.

Chapter 8

Restoring the Tabernacle of David

The scripture makes it crystal clear that we are living in the closing days of grace. First Chronicles 12:32 speaks of the children of Issachar *"which were men that had understanding of the times, to know what Israel ought to do...."* There is one universal need that permeates the body of Christ in these *last days*, a baptism of **discernment!** Discernment was Issachar's greatest asset; unfortunately, it seems to be the church's greatest deficiency at the moment. Discernment is needed because of the times and seasons during which we live. Without discernment the body of Christ is in grave danger of being overtaken by deceiving spirits and demonic doctrines (1 Timothy 4:1). Likewise, without proper discernment of the hour, we are also in danger of missing our moment of visitation (Luke 19:44). According to Numbers 2:5 and Numbers 10:14-15, there seems to be a direct correlation of praise and worship and discernment. The children of Issachar camped under the standard of Judah—praise--around the tabernacle.

Could it be that the children of Issachar developed their discernment out of their relationship with praise? It seems to me that a proper revelation of praise and worship is so important because it positions the church with discernment for the last days!

There were twelve stones on the breastplate of the High Priest; each stone represented one of the twelve tribes. Each stone was a different color, and each stone had the name of a tribe inscribed upon it. Issachar's stone was a sapphire. The sapphire is recorded twelve times in the Bible. It is a transparent gem with a variety of mineral corundum. The best-known variety of sapphires has blue tints, but sapphires do exist in all the colors of the rainbow. The sapphire is *second only to the diamond in hardness*. For this reason the stone is often used as an abrasive or *polishing agent!* Many scholars believe that the *sapphire represents the Lord's divine nature and His*

> **"It is in the process of being worshipped that God communicates His presence to men."**
> C.S. Lewis

holy character as seen in Exodus 24:10, Ezekiel 1:26, 10:1, and Revelation 21:19. In both Exodus and Ezekiel, the descriptions of sapphire under the Lord's feet signify that *the very foundation of all that the Lord does* is built upon His divine nature and holy character. It is the heritage of the saints of God to receive the sure mercies of David (Isaiah 55:3, Acts 13:34), including *protection from enemies* (Isaiah 54:17), the potential to become joint heirs (Romans 8:17), and *the opportunity to become the habitation of God* (Ephesians 2:22). The Spirit of Holiness (Psalm 89:34-36) confirmed this heritage to David. The heritage would also advance holiness in the hearts of those who would believe. It is evident in Isaiah 54:11 that the basic foundation of the house, represented by the sapphire, is the divine nature and holy character of God. It is only upon this same foundation of holiness and character that successful Christian living or ministry can result. In the mystery of Issachar's discerning abilities is the true power of worship:

☐ Worship develops a strong, tough spirit.

☐ Worship polishes the life of the believer.

☐ Worship reveals the nature and holiness of God's character.

- ☐ Worship is the foundation of the believer's walk with God.
- ☐ Worship provides protection from enemies.
- ☐ Worship creates a habitation for God.
- ☐ Worship gives the believer discernment of the times and seasons.

For those who have eyes to see and ears to hear and hearts to perceive, there is a tremendous move of the Holy Spirit that is promised to the world and to the church in the last days. At the present time, Jesus, the head of the church, is emphasizing specific spiritual truths to mature the church and to bring His church into proper spiritual alignment to *"...present it to Himself a glorious Church, not having spot, wrinkle, or any such thing; but that it should be holy and without blemish"* (Ephesians 5:27). One of the great emphases of the last days before the Lord's coming is the divine order of worship. Since man was created to worship, he has developed various forms that appealed to his particular spiritual, emotional and mental levels. Because of ignorance and lack of discernment about what and how God is moving in the area of worship in the last days, there is a real need to discover what the Word of God says about the matter. God promises that worship will be a major *key* to the last-day moving of the Spirit.

Acts 15:16 says, *"After this I will return and will rebuild the tabernacle of David, which has fallen down; I will rebuild its ruins and I will set it up...."* James was quoting directly from Amos 9:8-12 when he made this prophetic declaration. From this simple passage, a controversy has developed that basically falls into two interpretations. First, does the Tabernacle of David refer to the original establishment and future re-establishment of the Davidic Kingdom? Second, does it refer to an end-time emergence of the Davidic Order of Worship? Many say that this verse is speaking of the Davidic Kingdom only; and, in turn, they totally miss, reject, and neglect the Davidic Order of Worship. On the other hand, there are those who say that this passage refers only to the establishment of the Davidic Order of Worship; they, likewise, miss necessary truth concerning the re-establishment of the Davidic Kingdom.

Where Are My Keys?

Extensive research reveals that *both* the Davidic Kingdom and the Davidic Order of Worship are emerging in the earth during the final days of grace; therefore, this passage is speaking of both interpretations! Psalm 43:3 speaks of multiple tabernacles, *"O send out Thy light and truth; let them lead me; let them bring me unto Thy holy hill and to Thy tabernacles."* Psalm 84:1 again emphasizes multiple tabernacles, *"How amiable are thy tabernacle, O Lord of Hosts."* The Davidic throne cannot be separated from Davidic worship; they are divinely connected! David's selection to be king came as a result of his worship while he tended his father's sheep. His notoriety as a man of war resulting from his killing Goliath came because he despised Goliath's reproach of the God of Israel. His kingship is identifiable by the establishment of a simple tabernacle on Mt. Zion in which to house the Ark of the Covenant. All Israel watched as their king danced with all his might in worship as the Ark found its resting place on Zion. The book of Revelation describes the re-establishment of the future Davidic Kingdom as Jesus rules from the throne of David in Israel to which is connected the established throne of worship (Revelation 19)! The divine connection of the Davidic Kingdom and the Davidic Order of Worship opens the mystery of the *Key of David* (Revelation 3:7).

God promises the outpouring of His Spirit upon all flesh in the last days. This outpouring began in Acts 2 on the day of Pentecost; however, there is coming a day when the Holy Spirit will be poured out on all flesh as the former and the latter rain together in Israel. Beloved, Pentecost was just the beginning of the outpouring! The power of God's presence is coming upon all flesh in the last days. The purpose of the Tabernacle of David and the re-establishment of the Davidic Order of Worship are to usher in the outpouring of the Holy Ghost in the last days. It is not by chance that there is such an emphasis on worship and the discovery of the church's Jewish roots at the same time in modern Christendom. There is, in this hour, the merging of revelatory streams that are positioning the church with the *Key of David* for Kingdom work in the earth!

Possessing the *Key of David* is simply possessing an understanding of the power of praise and worship as it relates to the establishment of the Kingdom of God on this earth. The church must pattern worship after the Tabernacle of David. (This pattern will be discussed in the next chapter.) Davidic worship is the *key* to the harvest of nations. Acts 15 gives the account of Judaizing teachers of the Law of Moses who had come down from Jerusalem seeking to bring the believing Gentiles under the bondage of the Law. The purpose of the gathering

> **"Surely that which occupies the total time and energies of heaven must be a fitting pattern for earth."**
>
> Paul E. Billheimer

of the apostles and elders at Jerusalem was to discuss this matter. The Gentiles were coming to a saving faith in Jesus Christ, but the Judaizers wanted them to practice the observance of the Law. Vital issues were involved in this council meeting because the decisions of the apostles would affect the future of the New Testament Church and the relationship between Jews and Gentiles, specifically concerning faith in Christ. A careful study of Acts 15 makes it clear that the Judaizers were trying to bring the Gentiles under the order of the Tabernacle of Moses; that is, right standing with God through the Law, sacrificial systems, and works. They were teaching that only by means of circumcision, carnal ordinances, Aaronic priesthood, and sacrificial systems could one truly be a follower of God. Basically, the real question that was being asked at this council "What is the relationship of the Gentiles to the Mosaic Covenant as it relates to the Tabernacle of Moses?"

In Acts 15:7 Peter testified through his experience that the Lord poured out His Spirit on the Gentiles exactly as He had previously on the Jews at Pentecost. Paul and Barnabas corroborated that testimony in Acts 15:12, *"Then all the multitude kept silence, and gave audience to Barnabas and Paul, declaring what miracles and wonders God had wrought among the Gentiles by them."* James, by the word of wisdom, then stood and quoted the prophecy of Amos concerning the restoration of the Tabernacle of David, thereby, showing that the purpose of this outpouring was *"that the residue of men and all the Gentiles might seek after the Lord"* (Acts 15:15-17).

Throughout the worship order of David's Tabernacle, there is the *Key of David* which unlocks the harvest and establishes the Kingdom of God among the nations! Right now the fullness of the Gentiles (Romans 11:25) is upon the church. The Lord is raising up a people out of every tribe, tongue, kindred, and nation for His name's sake. According to Revelation 5:9-10, this remnant of believers shall stand before the throne of the Lamb singing new songs and playing instruments as they collectively worship Jesus after the order of David's Tabernacle!

Beloved, *these are the last days*! The church must grasp hold of the *Key of David*; Jesus said that He would give unto His church the *Keys of the Kingdom*. Worship is one of the primary keys that locks and unlocks the heavens. As did the children of Issachar, believers need a baptism of discernment to sense the present season and time. These are critical days, days filled with demonic activity in the world and in the church. As has been stated many times previously in this book, ***worship is a warfare tool***!

Worship is more than just a Sunday morning event; it is a *key to the harvest.* In the church that I pastor, we have found this *key!* Our people are consistently instructed about the power of praise and worship. They have been taught how the spiritual dynamics of true worship function and how the heavens respond. Because of their understanding of these truths, the *key* of worship is unlocking doors that no man can shut and shutting doors that no man can open. Many souls are converted and delivered every week--many during the worship time-- because the body of believers has discovered one of the *keys* to the kingdom. Guest ministers, small and great, leave our church awestruck by the power of praise and worship. The atmosphere of our church is electrified with faith, and the anointing is strong to set the captive free. Our sphere of influence is exponentially increasing on numerous fronts because both staff and congregation have found that the establishment of the kingdom in our region is directly linked to the passion of our worship!

Chapter 9

Breaking the Sound Barrier

With an understanding of the spiritual dynamics of worship and the emergence of the Tabernacle of David in the last days, we are ready to look at the kind of worship God likes and at why it is so important to be concerned with His particular taste more than with our own. With all of the modern worship wars that debate style and taste, many Christians have never taken the time to gain insight from the Word concerning the kind of worship God Himself enjoys. The purpose of the believer's life is to bring the Lord pleasure! *"You created everything, and it is **for your pleasure** that they exist and were created"* (NLT). We should be more concerned with what the King desires and enjoys than with what we desire and enjoy. Worship is not about us. It is about Him. When we make worship a

> **"The happiest man is he who learns from nature the lesson of worship."**
> Ralph Waldo Emerson

horizontal experience only, we remove power from worship.

As was the cross, worship is a crucible--a place or situation in which different elements interact to produce something new. Worship is primarily vertical in its expression. The purpose of worship is the connecting of earth with the heavens--deep calling unto deep. Although worship is essentially vertical, it has a horizontal expression as well. Jesus said, when asked what was the most important commandment in the Scripture, *"The first in importance is, Listen, Israel: The Lord your God is one; so love the Lord God with all your passion and prayer and intelligence and energy. And here is the second: Love others as well as you love yourself. There is no other commandment that ranks with these"* (Mark 12:29-31, The Message). In other words, our vertical position of worship, which expresses our love for God, directly affects our horizontal position in life, which is to love our neighbor as we love our self. God has promised His children that *"... He will give you all you need from day to day if you live for him and make the Kingdom of God your primary concern"* (Matthew 6:33, NLT*).*

To discover what and how God desires worship, we must look to the Tabernacle of David. Since God is restoring the Tabernacle of David in the last days, we can find God's style of worship within its curtains. First of all, David's Tabernacle was simple in its construction but powerful in its purpose. The Tabernacle operated for thirty-three years. This time span was a foreshadowing of Christ's earthly lifespan. He, veiled in human flesh, lived thirty-three years housing the glory of God. Worship through song and instrument day and night characterized David's tent; likewise, angels announced Jesus' birth with songs. Also, there was a sound from heaven as well at the birth of the church. There was a *sound* that resonated out of the structure where the hundred and twenty met that pleased the heart of God. It is the restoration of that same *sound* that is once again coming to the body of Christ. The Tabernacle of David was a place of unceasing *prayer, praise and proclamation*! To see this picture more clearly, we need to study the Psalms. In college I studied the Psalms only from a purely theological perspective. They are rich with theological truth; however, it never dawned on me that this book was primarily a *music* book until I went through a calamity that opened that door of revelation. When one studies Psalms from a *musical* perspective, an entirely different realm of revelation opens which is more than fascinating!

Do You Hear What I Hear?

Before we look at the musical aspect of the book of Psalms, we need to first establish the importance of *sound*. Within the body of Christ, little is understood about the power of *sound*– there is a need to break the *sound barrier* within the church. *Sound* matters to God—specifically, the *sounds* attached to the worship of God through songs and instruments. David understood something about the power of a song when he used certain styles of music to produce a specific *sound*. Sound is an interesting medium! Light travels at one hundred eighty-six thousand miles per second, the equivalence of seven and one-half times around the circumference of the earth in approximately one second.

Sound, on the other hand, travels at approximately seven hundred sixty-eight miles per hour, the equivalence of one mile in five seconds.

Although sound cannot travel at the speed of light, it can *bend the dimension of travel* and become light. For example, instruments are tuned to A-440 standard. At seven hundred octaves above A-440, sound turns into light which can be measured only by nanometers. A German physicist and musician Ernest Florens Friedrich Chladni made this discovery, along with many others discoveries concerning sound. His important works include research on vibrating plates and the calculation of the speed of sound for different gases. For these discoveries some call him the "Father of Acoustics" (*Wikipedia*). An example of sound's becoming light is found in some everyday applications. Wireless microphones convert sound into light which contacts a sound board that then converts it back to sound. Man's brain does the same thing with every conversation a man hears. When a sound is registered upon the eardrum through vibration, it is then translated into light pulses that interact within the brain. The scripture contains numerous passages that show the connection of sound and light (Genesis 1, Exodus 19:16, Psalms 77:18).

Dr. Carl Baugh of the Creation Research Museum believes that before the flood of Noah the firmament around the earth resonated with a sound that produced extraordinary plant and animal growth. Ezekiel, the prophet, seems to confirm this belief in his description of the earth before the fall (Ezekiel 1:14-27). It also seems that the original earth was filled with angelic activity which had a sound that resonated between the firmaments that encircled the earth. If this interpretation of scripture is correct, the pre-fall firmament above the earth acted as a tent that housed and amplified the acoustical effects of the worship coming from the angles. Imagine the earth in that state! Beloved, the new heaven and new earth will in the future once again become a place filled with the sounds of worship. Notice that in Ezekiel, as well as in many other scriptures, light in some form always accompanies the sounds being released.

On November 26, 1998, a BBC News report declared that the universe seems to be singing a collective song. They have found that even the Black Hole is emitting a sound. The Black Hole's giving forth a sound should be impossible because sound cannot travel through a vacuum--it must have a medium of travel. Nevertheless, the Black Hole, along with all the other heavenly bodies, is making a sound: *"The heavens declare the glory of God; and the firmament sheweth his handywork"* (Psalm 19:1). More recently, on October 21, 2005, *National Geographic* reported: "...your DNA is singing a song." The Harvard researcher Gil Alterovitz discovered that when the human genome is assigned specific notes, it seems to be playing a melody. What some scientist are now saying is that our DNA is nothing more than notes upon a scale and that our bodies are singing a song! According to an article in *Technology Review* entitled "The Body Is Out of Tune," when the music of a typical healthy strand of DNA is played, it sounds "soothing and harmonic." On the other hand, a diseased strand of DNA grows more dissonant as its signal becomes less healthy. Basically, scientists are discovering and predicting disease based on the sounds our bodies are making!

To take this one step further, scientists are trying to treat the body through "sound therapy"! They feel that certain frequencies have the ability to realign the melodies of the body, basically putting us back in tune! Maybe this is what God is doing; maybe He is retuning the body of Christ with the original sound of heaven that permeated the earth's atmosphere. This realignment sounds like the re-establishing of the Tabernacle of David in the earth. The worship in the Tabernacle of David was based on heaven's worship! In fact, Davidic worship always reappeared in every revival mentioned in the Old Testament. When the church comes into alignment with the *sounds* of heaven, there will be a mighty outpouring of God's Spirit in the earth. With every revival in world history, there emerged a specific sound that marked the moving of the Spirit. There is a new

> **"A glimpse of God will save you. To gaze at Him will sanctify you."**
>
> Manley Beasley

sound being released in the earth today. It is the sound of the Tabernacle of David!

What was the sound of David's Tabernacle? The majority of the Psalms were birthed out that tent. We do not realize just how much of a musical book that Psalms is. In the Psalms three individuals occur consistently-- *Heman, Asaph, Jeduthun.* First Chronicles chapters 15 and 16 identify these three people as the main directors of the Levitical ensembles. *Heman* was the *lead singer.* *Asaph* was the *choir director.* *Jeduthun,* also referred to as Ethan, was the *musical director.* Notice, everyone had his place in the Tabernacle based on his specific anointing. In the Psalms, usually at the beginning of each chapter, is an inscription that contains a name or a description for each Psalm. These headings are very important because they identify the type of sound that God likes in worship. Again, specific sounds are very important to God.

Skilled musicians and some lovers of music have noticed that certain songs seem to have more power in specific keys. Likewise, certain songs have different degrees of anointing based on the instruments or the vocalists involved. David understood this *key* about worship. He had a sense of *sound,* and he knew how to create it for particular situations or needs. He demonstrated this knowledge when his worship and skillful playing calmed the evil spirits that tormented Saul. As every worship leader prepares to lead worship, he needs to seek God about specific keys, colors, vocalists, instruments, and styles. All of these factors in combination are *keys* to releasing a sound that pleases the heart of God and produces a symphony between heaven and earth.

Notice how specific each Psalm is about style and specific sounds. For example, the inscription for Psalm four reads: *"To the chief Musician on **Neginoth**, A Psalm of David." Neginoth* means *stringed instruments.* In other words, this particular song has an anointing on it when played with stringed instruments. Psalm five's inscription says, *"To the chief Musician upon **Nehiloth**, A Psalm of David." Nehiloth* is a word which describes flutes and other wind instruments. Again, David is instructing the chief Musician (i.e. Jeduthun, Asaph, or Heman) that this

Psalm must be accompanied by wind instruments to create the desired atmosphere of worship and praise. Psalms six and twelve are songs that must be put to a specific type of stringed instrument, an eight-stringed lyre. According to 1 Chronicles 15:20, there were eight harp players who worshipped in the Tabernacle of David.

Psalms 8, 81, and 84 speak of an instrument of *Gath*. The *Targum*, an ancient Aramaic paraphrase or interpretation of the Hebrew Bible, states that David brought an instrument from Gath after killing Goliath of Gath. This action is powerful! David saw the value of taking an instrument out of the world's or enemy's hands and redeeming it for worship to God. The church should not be allowing the world to steal our musicians. On the other hand, there are some sounds that the world currently possesses that need to be redeemed and brought into the church for worship. Psalm 22 is a song that was set to a specific melody of Israel. David simply used a known melody and put faith-filled worship words to it.

In Psalm 39 and 1 Chronicles 16:42, Jeduthun was playing percussion instruments. In Psalm 39 it seems that, based on the inscription, this song was set to percussion-driven worship. Wonder how those who do not like drums in church reckon that? Psalm 46 was sung in a specific style, *Alamoth*. Alamoth is a phrase that means--young women. More than likely this Psalm, this particular song, was to be sung in falsetto by the women's chorus.

Again, David had a unique understanding about the power of music, worship, and sound. The church needs to *break the sound barrier*! There is a new sound that God desires to release in the body of Christ right now. With the release of that new sound, will come a fresh anointing that will break forth in a powerful revival. The church needs to take worship out of the religious box and explore the sounds of the Spirit realm. Worship is not about a specific style or taste; it is about discovering what brings God pleasure. Ephesians 5:19 and Colossians 3:16 teaches what authentic New Testament worship really is. It is *psalms, hymns, and spiritual songs*. The word *psalm* means to *strike or twang a musical instrument.* GOD LIKES MUSICAL INSTRUMENTS OF ALL TYPES! The word *hymn* is derived from the Greek word *humnos* which means the songs of heroes or sacred songs. GOD LIKES IT WHEN WE SING THE OLD SONGS OF THE FOREFATHERS OF OUR FAITH! The phrase spiritual songs in the Greek is *pneumatikos* which means an unrehearsed spirit. GOD LIKES US TO SING SONGS INSPIRED BY THE HOLY SPIRIT THAT ARE UNREHEARSED AND SPONTANEOUS! Paul teaches in First Corinthians 14 that we should be singing in the Spirit, which is unknown tongues and spiritual utterances. Until believers take worship out of the church box and pursue the pleasure of God as the highest aim of worship, the sound of heaven can never be released in the earth! *The church needs to break the sound barrier!*

Chapter 10

Symphony of Earth

As stated in previous chapters, worship is essentially spiritual. Worship is not about a style or place. It is primarily vertical in its focus upon the Godhead. There is more happening in worship than we could ever imagine. Hopefully, you realize by now that there are powerful spiritual dynamics occurring through worship; however, heaven will reveal that there is much more than is discussed in this book. We have learned that the angels are very active during worship and are attending our worship services. Also, we have discovered that "where two or three are gathered" that Jesus is in their midst. We have also learned, according to Hebrews 1:11-12, that Jesus is active in our midst through His declarations of the redemptive names of God to the brethren and by even joining the church in singing praises to the Father.

Our understanding about the *warfare of worship* has increased as well. Exodus 32 makes it crystal clear that worship sounds like warfare to the heavens. When we worship, there is an assembling of spiritual entities to the sound of warfare. However, this passage also teaches us that we must be careful not to be ritualistic in our worship. Spiritual forces understand the sounds of *true worship*. Greater revelation about Satan's original role upon the earth as a worshipping being, his downfall, his loss of the anointing of authority, and the creation of man as Satan's replacement as a worshipping being clarifies the spiritual struggle all believers have concerning worship. Wickedness is an intense enemy of the power of worship in the life of a true believer!

Through the warfare of worship and by our taking our rightful place as worship instruments, we have the pathway to dominion. We understand that spiritual authority is established *in* and *through* true worship. Judah—*praise--goes first*. Praise chokes the necks of our enemies and destroys the yokes that bind us. Praise is a beautiful, powerful garment that removes the spirits of heaviness and oppression!

Although we have been created with the power of worship within as was Lucifer, we must be careful not to allow that power to be corrupted in any way. We must not betray our Lord, as did Judas, with the *kiss of worship.* Protecting the purity of worship through holy living and proper spiritual alignment must be a priority with every worshipper. For those of us who are anointed as worship leaders and spiritual authorities, we dare not *merchandise* our anointing for personal gain or recognition. Spiritual leaders have a responsibility to protect our flocks from those malcontents, disguised as sheep, who seek to rape the spiritual landscapes by *merchandised* worship.

The power of pure worship provokes a response in the heavens. The Godhead is active around the throne when worshippers offer pure, spiritual worship. Zephaniah teaches that God sings and dances under strong emotion as He responds to His children's cries. The angels stand amazed in the heavens at the Lord's response to His beloved as He releases His love songs over the church. His response is the reason that it is so important for us to worship in the ways that bring pleasure to the Lord. We discover the *tastes* of God by studying the Tabernacle of David. Within its humble curtains, the sounds of *prayer, praise and proclamation* were being released continuously. God promises to restore the power of the Davidic Order of worship in the last days. Accompanying this revelation of worship will be a powerful move of the Holy Spirit in the earth that will bring in a harvest of souls.

The church will discover and unleash new *sounds*! These *new sounds* will be discovered and unleashed so that *"...the manifold wisdom of God might now be made known through the church to the rulers and the authorities in the heavenly places"* (Ephesians 3:10). Beloved, there is a convergence of heaven and earth taking place right now! The Kingdom is coming to earth as it is in heaven! We, the body of Christ, must prepare ourselves for God's final agenda in the earth because He has always chosen to do His finest work through His church.

The New Wine Is in the Cluster

The word *symphony* is a compelling word. *Symphony* comes from three words: *sum, fonay, and phaino. Sum* means *with; fonay* means *a tone* or *sound,* and *phaino* means *to cause to shine* and *bring forth light.* In Matthew 18:19 there is a word which means symphony, *"Again I say to you, that if two of you agree on earth about anything that they may ask, it shall be done for them by My Father who is in heaven."* The word *agree* is the Greek word *sumphoneo,* the English equivalent is *symphony.* In summation, symphony is the agreement of tones or sounds that cause to shine and bring forth light! This passage is saying that when there is an agreement on the earth among believers, there is a *symphony* of sound released that provokes a sound from heaven. This convergence of sounds causes a breaking forth of light into the darkness of earth. Beloved, this is what the Lord is doing in the earth right now!

As I travel the nation and the world, I am seeing the convergence of sounds from every denomination, tribe, tongue, and kindred. The harmonies of Christ's various body parts converging to make one sound is releasing a new anointing in the earth for this final hour! Isaiah says that the *new wine* is in the cluster. Psalm 133 echoes this truth by stating that there is a priestly anointing released upon the unity of believers. Only the Levites were allowed to carry the Ark of the Covenant. *Levi* means *joined*! The glory of the Lord can be made fully known to the world only when the body of Christ comes together with an agreement of tones (Ephesians 4:11-13). We do not have to sing in unison, but we must sing in harmony! We do not have to cease to be distinctive, but we must refuse to be divisive!

The greatest need for the body of Christ is to discover our corporate ability. Individual worship is powerfully effective; however, it is not nearly so effective as corporate worship! David was anointed in three dimensions. First, he was anointed as a shepherd to be the King of Israel. He had to learn how to handle his individual anointing before he could operate in the manifestation of his kingly anointing. He was anointed in the midst of his brethren when only God could see his potential. Then, he was anointed king over Judah. It was this third-dimension anointing that gave him partial authority over the future consolidated nation. During this time he learned from Saul what *not* do as a leader of men. Finally, David was anointed King over all Israel in Hebron. Hebron translated means *confederation or unity*. The greatest anointing was for the unifying of the nation. The church's greatest anointing will come only when the body of Christ, the "perfect man in the earth," stands up in unity.

There is power in diversity. The sound of instruments or voices in unison does not have nearly the power that those same voices or instruments have when in perfect harmony. Beloved, God is creating a divine symphony in the earth. Streams of ministry are converging for such a time as this to release the sound of heaven in the earth! I have found that when sermons cannot get people together a song can. Worship will be one of the essential unifying factors for the Church in the last days!

Worship is a powerful weapon in the arsenal of the believer. Just as do the angels, take your heavenly flight with the wings of worship around the throne and discovery the innumerable facets of God's unspeakable glory! The greatest desire in the heart of God is to be known by man. Man's greatest need is to know God. Worship is the vehicle of intimacy. It always has been, and it always will be. Worship should be the most natural thing in the world for the Christian! To worship God is the reason for man's creation!

Do You Know Jesus?

The Bible says, "That if thou shalt confess with thy mouth the Lord Jesus, and shalt believe in thine heart that God hath raised Him from the dead, thou shalt be saved," (Romans 10:9). Pray this prayer from your heart today! "Dear Jesus, I believe that You died for me and rose again on the third day. I confess I am a sinner...I need Your love and forgiveness...Come into my heart. Forgive my sins. I receive Your eternal life. Confirm Your love by giving me peace, joy and supernatural love for others. Amen."

Yes, Pastor Shane! I made a decision to accept Christ as my personal Savior today. Please send me my free devotional book: **The Word For You Today**.

NAME_____BIRTHDAY___/___/___
ADDRESS_____
CITY_____STATE _____
ZIP _____   PHONE _____
EMAIL _____

Please Mail To: First Assembly, 715 Cypress St.
West Monroe, La 71291
Email: info@firstassemblywm.org
For prayer support please call 318-387-1500

Who is Shane Warren?

Pastor Shane Warren was called to preach at the age of twelve through a supernatural visitation. After preaching his first message at twelve, he continued to passionately pursue God and his ministry call throughout his teenage years. In 1991, he graduated from Lee University with a B.A., in Theology and B.S., in Education. His unique, dynamic ability to communicate a relevant word has made him a sought-after speaker and teacher. His prophetic insight, revelation, and heart for the lost has blessed him with the opportunity to minister to pastors and congregations alike worldwide through leadership conferences, retreats, church growth seminars, mentoring programs, crusades, and church strife resolutions. His burden for the lost and for mentoring men and women of God is the driving force behind his ministry. He is respected inter-denominationally for his teaching, preaching, and church growth philosophies. Pastor Warren is a published author. He serves as the president of The Voice Network, a television station. He speaks abroad, and serves as the Senior Pastor of First Assembly of God in West Monroe, Louisiana, where he resides with his wife Pam and son Adam.

For more information on speaking invitations or additional resources by Pastor Warren, please contact him at the following address:

Shane Warren

715 Cypress St.

West Monroe, La 71291

Phone: 318-387-1500

Email: pastorshane@firstassemblywm.org

NOTES

Secrets of the Well

Shane Warren

NOTES

_____

_____

_____

_____

_____

_____

_____

_____

_____

_____

_____

_____

_____

_____

_____

_____

_____

_____

_____

Secrets of the Well

Shane Warren

NOTES

Secrets of the Well

Shane Warren

NOTES

_____

_____

_____

_____

_____

_____

_____

_____

_____

_____

_____

_____

_____

_____

_____

_____

_____

_____

_____

_____

Secrets of the Well

Shane Warren

NOTES

Secrets of the Well

Shane Warren